```
791.43    Manchel, Frank
Ma
     When pictures began
       to move
```

DATE DUE			
MAY 16.1983			

DEMCO 38-297

when pictures began to move

by Frank Manchel

Illustrated with photographs

Line drawings by James Caraway

Prentice-Hall, Inc., Englewood Cliffs, N.J.

WHEN PICTURES BEGAN TO MOVE by Frank Manchel

© 1969 by Frank Manchel
© 1969 by Prentice-Hall, Inc., for illustrations in this edition

All rights reserved. No part of this book may be reproduced in any form or by any means, except for the inclusion of brief quotations in a review, without permission in writing from the publisher.

13–955336–3

Library of Congress Catalog Card Number: 69–17633

Printed in the United States of America • J

Prentice-Hall International, Inc., London
Prentice-Hall of Australia, Pty. Ltd., Sydney
Prentice-Hall of Canada, Ltd., Toronto
Prentice-Hall of India Private Ltd., New Delhi
Prentice-Hall of Japan, Inc., Tokyo

Second Printing . . . . January, 1971

contents

FILM BEGINNINGS 1

A TRICK OR TREAT BUSINESS 12

A TRUST CREATED 23

THE FIRST GIANTS 31

THE CHANGING TIMES 44

THE RUSSIAN WORKSHOP 52

THE MAD GENIUSES 59

THE SILENT HOURS 70

BIBLIOGRAPHY 72

INDEX 75

To Robbie Wachtel

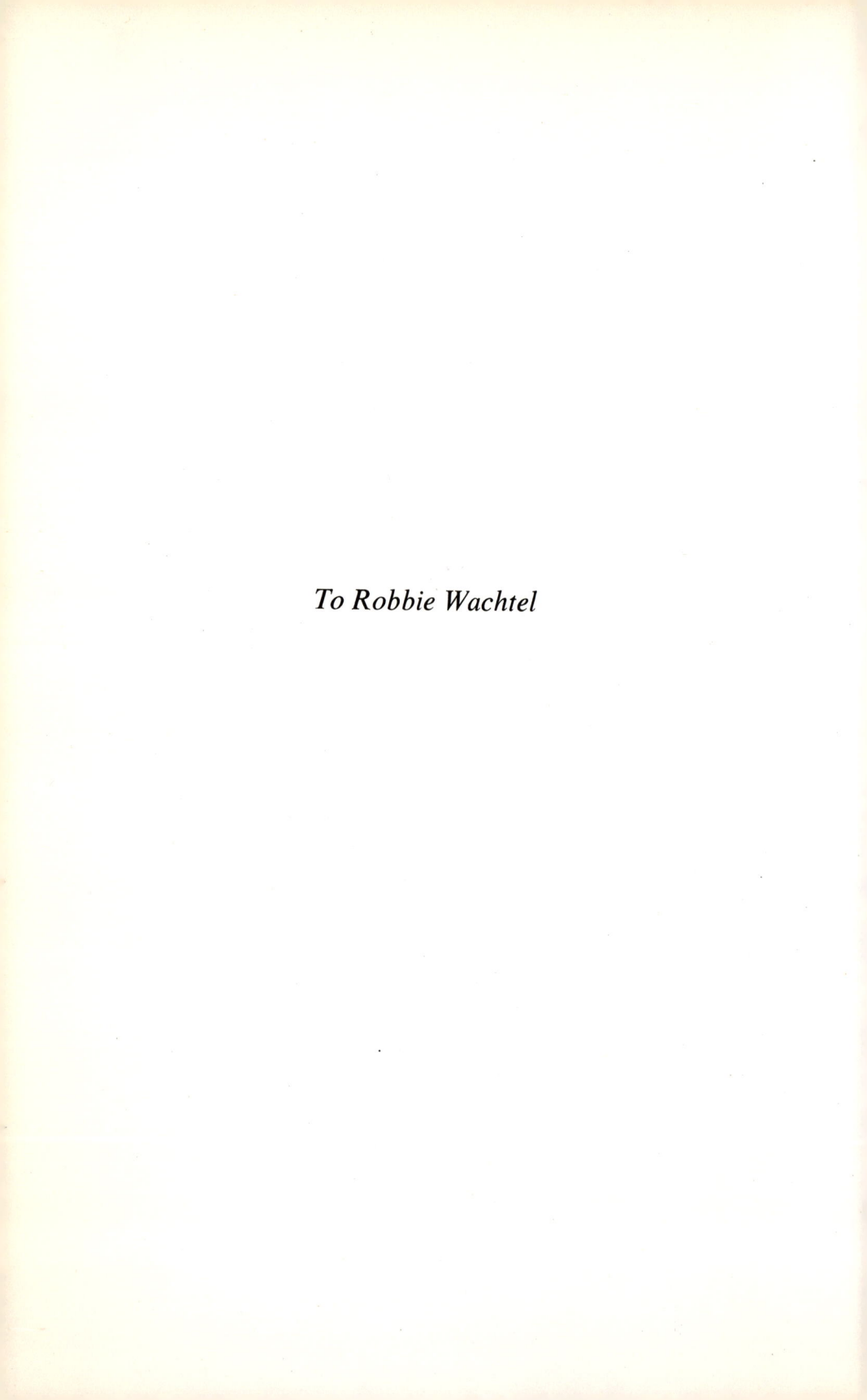

FILM BEGINNINGS

You walk into a darkened auditorium, sit in a comfortable seat and stare up at the large wide silver screen. Shortly, you might begin to watch a jungle man swinging through the trees, or a rocket ship reaching for the stars, or a wagon train of settlers heading toward a new frontier.

You know that what you are watching is sheer fantasy, yet it seems so lifelike. You even feel that you're part of the great adventure. That is the power of the cinema. That is why movies are one of the most exciting and important art forms in the world today.

This book is about how motion pictures began. It is about the early days when bold, talented and unprincipled individuals helped to create, organize and develop the film industry to the stage where today billions of people go to the movies each month.

Sadness, confusion and dishonesty are the keynotes of the initial years. No one knows who first thought of making pictures move. No one is certain where the work actually began, and no one knows who really deserves the credit. This much we do know: many men, over a period of years, worked on the idea. Through it all, coincidences, mistakes, cheating, hunches and experiments marked the road to success.

As we go back in history, we find that philosophers, scientists, con-men, clergymen and inventors contributed to the story. These great and strange men, using mostly hand-drawn pictures, worked with mirrors, prisms and lenses to imitate lifelike movement. They didn't succeed. The materials were too primitive, and the results, too unnatural.

For the most part, the problems remained the same. First, how many successive pictures were required to create the impression of motion? Second, how could these pictures be related to each other? Third, how could these pictures be seen or projected? Fourth, at what speed should these pictures be shown? In addition, there were the problems of constructing a machine to record the pictures and another to show them. None of the problems could be solved before the coming of electricity.

That didn't stop people from claiming to have found the answers. Probably the most famous legend is that a mathematician, Father Athanasius Kircher, produced in the mid-1640's in Rome the first movies with his magic lantern. This unorthodox cleric also had another title, the "doctor of a hundred arts." Kircher's "work" involved drawing images on glass slides, placing these slides on a movable rod in front of a lantern in a dark room, and having the images flashed on the opposite wall. Even if the reports were true, this method would not produce moving pictures, but merely one picture substituting for another.

The point is that pictures remained, for the most part, immobile until a major breakthrough in the nineteenth cen-

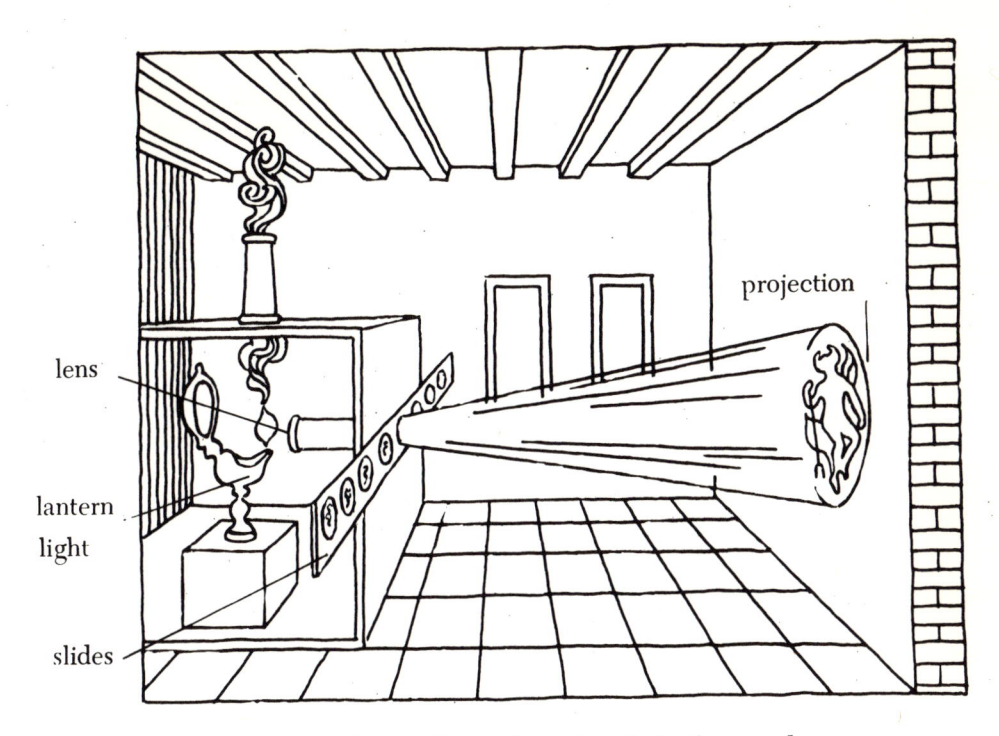

Father Kircher's "magic lantern" consisted of a lamp, a lens, and a series of pictures that were projected on the opposite wall. As you can see, these were not moving pictures, but changing slides.

tury. In 1824, in London, Peter Mark Roget helped solve the problem, discussed more than 1800 years before by the Greek mathematician Ptolemy, concerning the persistence of vision. Roget's explanation, simply put, stated that there is a curious defect in human sight. When the human eye sees an image, it retains an impression of that image on the retina for close to a tenth of a second *after* the image itself changes or disappears.

The importance of this fundamental theory to motion pictures was demonstrated by two scientists working independently of each other: Joseph Antoine Ferdinand Plateau in Brussels and Simon Ritter von Stampfer in Vienna. Plateau's experiments with handmade drawings and revolving discs

rotating metal drum

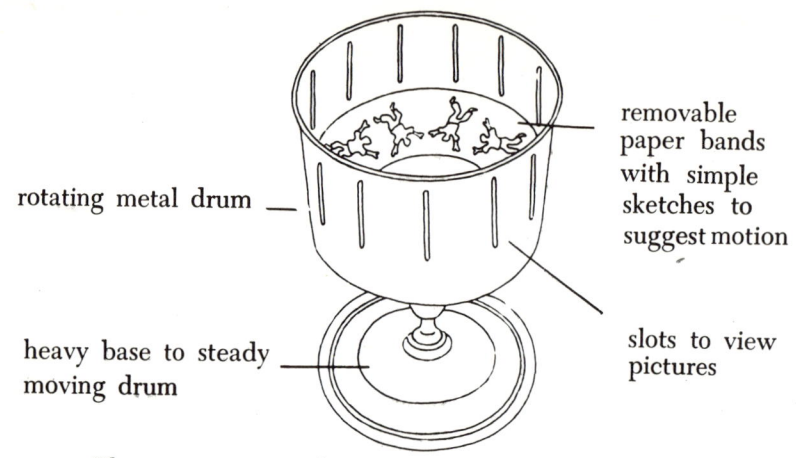

removable paper bands with simple sketches to suggest motion

heavy base to steady moving drum

slots to view pictures

The zoetrope is a slot-punctured rotating metal drum that comes complete with paper bands which match the circumference of the drum, but are only half the depth. Each one has a series of consecutive movements by a figure, and as the drum rotates, the viewer has the illusion of action drawings.

were similar, coincidently, to Stampfer's. By using a series of shots of a particular action shown consecutively in a second, these men were able to create the illusion of motion. The eye was unable to see the pictures changing. (Tragically, Plateau's dedication to his optical research caused him to go blind in 1844.)

Quickly, inventors and promoters began to bring out devices to test the principle. The truth was obvious in their various machines, which amounted to little more than childish toys: spinning wheels, revolving discs, moving tops, and thumb-flipped picture books.

One such device was the zoetrope, often referred to as the "Wheel of Life," since the action drawings centered on such well-known scenes as a child skipping rope, or a man pumping water. The method of presentation involved mounting a series of successive drawings of figures performing a single motion onto a paper cylinder inside a revolving drum. The outside wall had equidistant slots for viewing the action. The slots acted just as the soon-to-be-discovered shutter, allowing the viewer to see the pictures only fifty percent of the time and thus maintaining the illusion of motion. Since the bands were detachable, the spectator could change his shows whenever he desired.

In practical terms, these novelties were worthless. They offered little chance for prolonged stories. They could not effectively maintain the illusion of motion very long. Few people could watch the action at one time. And they were very expensive not only to make, but also to supply with films.

A group of scientists were already at work trying to find some way of reducing the long and tedious hours that went into producing the hand drawings. A major contribution was made by two Parisians: Joseph Nicéphore Niépce and Louis Jacques Mandé Daguerre. In the 1820's, these two pioneers combined their efforts to probe the possibilities of certain silver compounds, sensitized glass plates and sunlight. Tragedy struck again: Niépce died five years before the final process was completed. Then, in 1838, Daguerre dramatically demonstrated his photographic process, and the result, the daguerreotype, a permanent record of actual images. True, he

In the early days of photography the subject was kept motionless by clamps (called a head rest) attached to the back of his head.

could only produce a single picture, and the subject had to remain motionless for fifteen minutes. But as a result of this very significant process, drawings were no longer the only reproductions that had to be used with moving pictures.

Now what was needed was a camera and a method for taking pictures of actual motion. The glass plate process had too many drawbacks to be the final solution. Not only were the plates too heavy, but they were extremely fragile.

The problem, therefore, was how to connect photography with the illusion of moving pictures. Again, no one person can be given the credit for solving the question. Two names, however, dominate the discussion: Eadweard Muybridge and Étienne-Jules Marey. Legend has it that Muybridge became involved in the issue because he was a professional photographer called in by Governor Leland Stanford of California to settle a bet. The Governor stubbornly argued that when a race horse galloped, its four feet left the ground. Someone else foolishly bet him that it wasn't so. Being a wealthy man, the Governor was determined to settle the issue. In 1877, Muybridge and an engineer John D. Isaacs sectioned off a stretch of race track and covered it with twenty-four threads. These threads, in turn, were attached to the triggers of twenty-four cameras. As the horse galloped past the cameras, tripping the threads, photography recorded how the horse's four hoofs left the track.

After that, Muybridge spent all his time photographing motion of any type. His purpose was primarily to make money, but his value to movies lay in his ability to create interest in the possibilities of recording moving pictures.

Marey, on the other hand, was a scientist interested in the theoretical possibilities of cameras. By studying the photographing experiments of others, he produced in 1882 a portable photographic gun. Briefly, Marey applied Plateau's idea of a revolving disc to shooting successive images. The cameraman placed the gun to his shoulder, pulled the trigger, and

plate rotated and stopped by claws

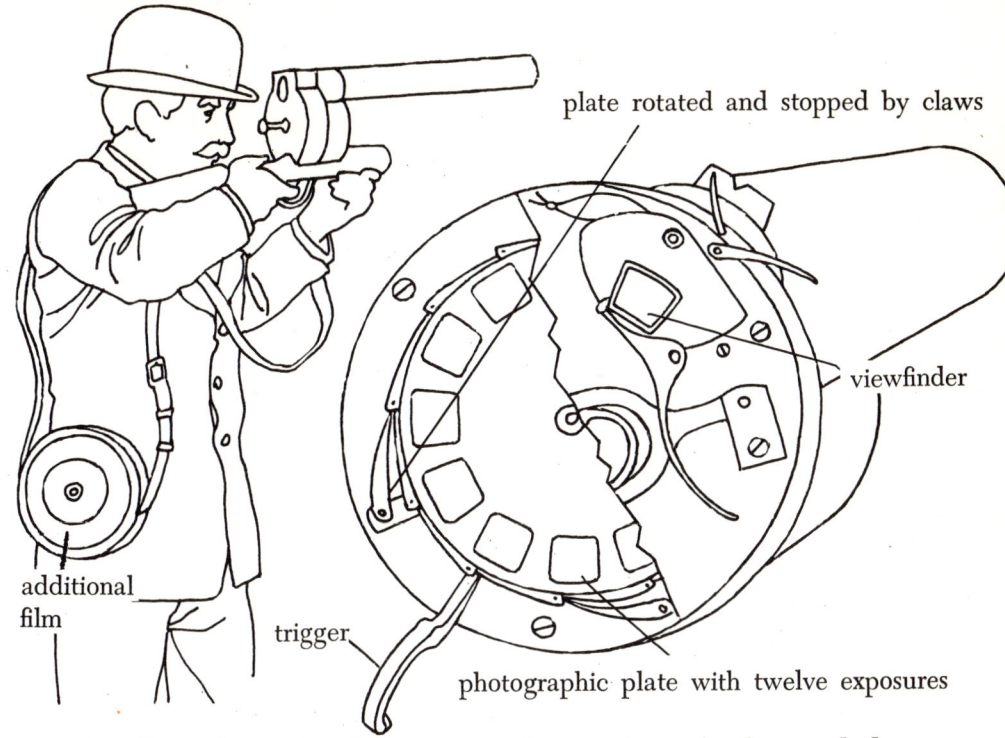

viewfinder

additional film

trigger

photographic plate with twelve exposures

the glass plate cartridges put on the turning wheel recorded the motion. Later on, he modified his approach in favor of rolls of celluloid film. Probably very few men in the early days of movies contributed as much as Marey to studying and defining the problems that later innovators would need to solve.

By the late 1800's the Reverend Hannibal Williston Goodwin had discovered the value of an emulsion base for photography. Working with this idea, George Eastman and his associates successfully combined fusel oil and amyl acetate (banana oil) to the elements of celluloid. The result: a film which was strong, transparent and flexible. Unfortunately, Goodwin was not given credit or cash for his work. Years later, his family received a five-million-dollar court settlement but it hardly made up for the profit that could have been his.

During these days, inventors also made important progress with lenses, reels of film, and perforated celluloid.

Crucial to all this progress was the concept of intermittent motion. In short, the idea was to move the celluloid from the supply reel, past the lens where the shutter opened and the light projected the image, and then on to the take-up reel. Basically, the plan called for film with perforated holes that could be jerked along by a spinning spur wheel. Audiences were not particularly happy with the first such machines, primarily because the jerking movements almost always caused flickering or breakage of the film.

The stage was set for two men to synthesize all the other efforts: William Dickson and Thomas Edison. Dickson had the ideas and Edison had the organization. From their efforts in Edison's workshop in West Orange, New Jersey, came the forerunner of the movies: the Kinetoscope. This was a machine with fifty feet of enclosed celluloid film mounted on two spools. All one had to do was drop a coin in a slot and look through an opening at the top of the box. An electric light flashed on the film inside, while a tiny motor moved the spools of film. The viewer, staring through the peep-hole, saw miniature human beings in action: for example, a man sneezing, a snake dancer wiggling, a couple of men fighting, or a baby getting washed.

Edison's phonograph parlors, set up to demonstrate his "talking machine" discovered in 1878, were reconverted to include his moving picture novelty. These places soon became known as penny arcades, where people came to watch the peep shows which ran for about a minute each.

Those who saw the moving figures were delighted. But Edison was unimpressed with the potential of movies. To him, they were still a toy. He agreed to patent the machine in the United States. He would not, however, spend another few hundred dollars to safeguard his rights in Europe. This was a mistake which not only cost him billions of dollars, but was also soon to haunt him.

There were other men who had greater vision. They realized that a fortune was to be had if someone could perfect a

Even after the success of screen projection, many movie parlors such as this one in 1896 continued to advertise the phonograph with the Kinetoscope. (Note the women at the right using ear plugs to hear the recordings.)

THE BETTMANN ARCHIVE

machine which enabled the film to be removed from the box and projected onto a screen where many people could view it at once. An important step forward was taken by the Latham family when they helped solve the problem of film movement through the projectors and cameras. In essence, the Lathams recognized that film breakage occured when the film was jerked from the supply reel to its position in front of the lens. The tension was too great and the tug too strong. By adding an extra spur or sprocket to the wheel, however, the film did not move to the lighting stage first but formed a loop or slack position in the movement through the machine.

Thus, when the wheel needed to change frames, the jerk was made on a loose celluloid, thereby reducing the force of the pull. This technique, known as "the Latham Loop," figured prominently in the patent fights of future years.

Another important innovation was the discontinuing of continuously moving celluloid. Men like Thomas Armat and Charles Francis Jenkins argued that flickering, erratic gestures and poor illumination were the result of an improper projection mechanism. Their contribution to film development was a stop-start-stop system of intermittent motion. To put it another way, the ingenious plan (based largely on Swiss watch movements) was to have each frame rest for a given period of time in front of the lens so that a definite impression would be made on the audience. Before and after such a long rest, the film would make short jumps from the supply reel to the take-up reel. This considerably reduced the annoying flickering effects of the early movies as well as improving the illusion of movement.

Edison still considered the motion picture projector unimportant.

In Europe, Englishmen, Germans, and Frenchmen took advantage of Edison's unguarded machine. The most brilliant innovators were Auguste and Louis Lumière. They perfected their own gearshift action, which at the same time reduced the number of pictures needed to maintain the persistence of vision from forty to sixteen.

Finally, on March 22, 1895, in the Lumière factory at Lyon, the Lumière brothers showed a newsreel account of their employees during a lunch break. Many historians consider this to be the first authentic movie showing in history.

Edison finally got the idea. By buying the rights, he combined the Latham loop with the Armat-Jenkins gearshift mechanism to manufacture a projector called the Vitascope (from the Latin word "vita," meaning "life," and the Greek ending "scope," meaning "look at").

The Lumières scored a hit at their first public showing with shots of employees leaving the brothers' factory.
THE MUSEUM OF MODERN ART/FILM STILLS ARCHIVE

And on April 23, 1896, in New York City on the spot where Macy's now stands, motion pictures were shown for the first time publicly in the United States. After the audience recovered from the spectacular impact, they screamed for the inventor so that they could shower him with honor. No one came forward. No one should have. No one person had been responsible.

A TRICK OR TREAT BUSINESS

Looking back on the 1890's, we can see that there were several ingredients which made movies an early success: opportunity, coincidence, and entertainment. No one can deny the great contributions of the inventors with their novel devices. These creative individuals experimenting with sight, sound, color, animation, photographic processes and mechanical equipment pointed the way to future technological achievements.

But we need to remember that the production methods used in those infant days were very crude by present standards. A case in point was Edison's film studio, The Black Maria, which cost less than seven hundred dollars to construct. This tarpapered building had a portion of the roof which could be removed on sunny days for lighting purposes. The interior of the building consisted mainly of a black background and a studio floor set on a circular track which was rotated during the filming (shooting) so that the main force of the sun's rays could be used at all times. The finished results were also crude. The first movies ran for just one reel, had only 960 separate pictures (frames), and could be used only a few times before they had to be discarded.

Remember also that the camera technique was very limited and editing was unheard of. The shooting of the "one reelers" was done from a single position and distance, and the final print closely resembled the action of a stage play: opening with an entrance and closing with a climax, focusing for the most part on a single scene, and using exaggerated stage gestures. Most important, the movies reflected the fact that the

In addition to his Black Maria, Edison maintained luxurious studios in New York. Notice how silent films enabled directors to make several pictures at the same time.
THE MUSEUM OF MODERN ART/FILM STILLS ARCHIVE

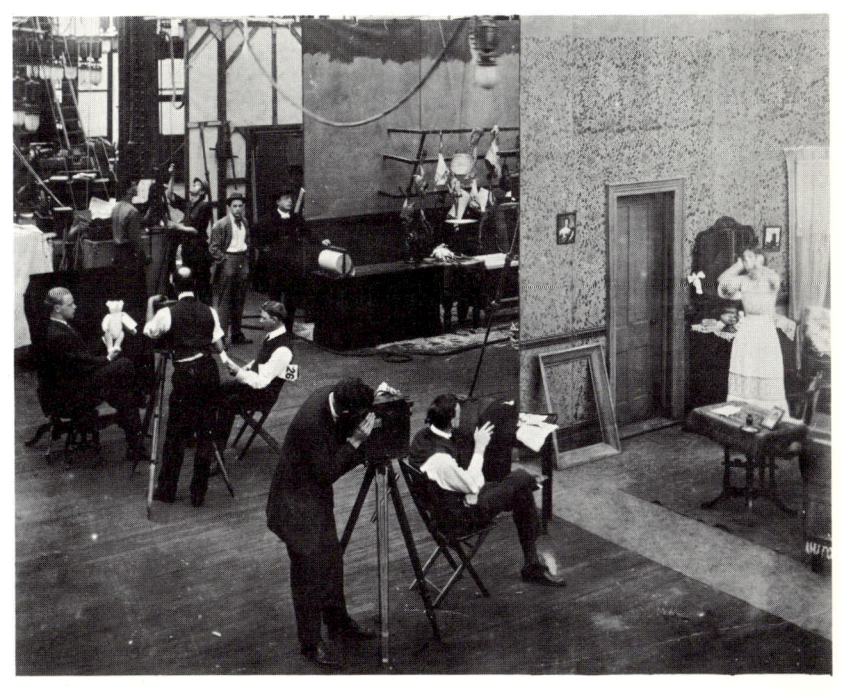

owners were interested in one main idea: how to make money quickly. Thus, the moving pictures were made like mass-produced products, so many movies were turned out per day.

There was another possible explanation for the close relationship between the cinema and the theater. Motion pictures, to summarize briefly, were the outgrowth of a stage tradition of romanticism and realism that had started a hundred years before. At that time, theatrical people began emphasizing the need for excitement and lifelike situations in drama. No matter what melodrama or comedy was performed, the producers worked on making the stage appear natural. Consequently, the old method of using painted backgrounds was replaced by make-believe mountains, fairy tale forests, and decorated sets. Stage designers constructed all manner of machines which could help maintain the illusion of reality. By the time movies were born, therefore, people were very much interested in pictorial realism.

Furthermore, this stage tradition had two handicaps which movies did not have. One was the problem of the bulky, expensive theatrical equipment which required a large stage. Since only the large cities could afford to maintain adequate theaters, many people only heard about the spectacular performances. Second, the expense of performing these exciting productions required high admission prices, again limiting the number of people who could go to the theater. Movies, on the other hand, presented realistic, romantic and spectacular scenes simply and economically for all who wanted to come.

Here too was another reason for the early success of movies. Men like Edison knew how to capitalize on the social nature of the new toy. They sensed that moving pictures appealed to a new audience of poor and young people, particularly the immigrant class. For those who could not read, write, or speak English, the silent movies with simple titles became their major means of entertainment. Anyone who could see, could go. What's more, you could go often: the admission was only a nickel.

Thomas Edison (1847-1931) shown with an early camera in 1893.
THE BETTMANN ARCHIVE

Nickelodeons, as the first projection houses were called, sprouted quickly after 1896; first in basements and back rooms, then in store fronts, hotels, factories and convention halls. There would have been even more if the equipment wasn't so scarce and expensive. When the movies were taken over by the vaudeville houses and featured as a star attraction, the future looked very bright indeed. Even though the films showed the same song-and-dance routines as the stage show, the sensation of seeing people move who were ten times normal size thrilled the audience.

Although business was good, promoters like Edison and the Lumière brothers felt that the fad of moving pictures would soon pass. But there were others who thought differently. To them, here was a golden opportunity to cash in on a scientific toy. Pool hall proprietors, theatrical agents, magicians, salesmen, medicine men and their show business buddies began to drift into the movie set-up. No matter where they came from, these operators shared several common characteristics: aggressiveness, a belief that movies could make them a fortune, and very little money of their own. This new breed had little concern for ethics and even less regard for good taste. Anything was okay as long as it resulted in a profit. For all those questionable traits, if it hadn't been for these men there would probably have been no movie industry.

A good example of their methods was the practice of "duping." For the first few years of the movies, the exhibitors had to buy every film they showed. The new breed of moviemakers didn't bother making their own films. They didn't have the time or the money. Instead, they would buy a popular film at the regular price and then send someone down into a basement to make several new prints or "pirated" copies. These duped prints were then sold for less than the original price. Another practice, once movies could be rented instead of bought, was to pay the price for showing the film at one

One of the first movies was a film in 1895 of Auguste Lumière feeding his daughter breakfast. The Lumières produced at the same time a slapstick comedy entitled *L'Arroseur arrose (A Practical Joke on the Gardener).*

THE BETTMANN ARCHIVE

theater and then hire a person to bicycle the print to other local movie houses.

But by 1900, the public appeared to be dissatisfied with the obvious repetition of movement for movement's sake. The vaudeville houses no longer put movies in prime spots, but instead used the moving pictures as "chasers" to get people to leave so that new customers could be brought in. And the cost and scarcity of the equipment still continued to discourage the growth of more theaters. It seemed as if the novelty of movies was wearing off.

Suddenly, the cinema found new life. The vaudeville managers and the actors got into a fight with each other over salaries. The performers formed a union called "The White Rats" and one of their first decisions was to call a strike. The managers had three choices: meet the union's demands, close their expensive theaters, or . . . show only movies. They gambled with showing just movies. And it worked. People flocked to the song-and-dance houses.

The demand for projectors became tremendous, and projection production went into full swing. Then, before anyone realized what was happening, the strike ended, leaving the manufacturers overstocked with expensive equipment and facing financial ruin. While this was a bad situation for the manufacturers, it turned out to be a splendid opportunity for anyone who wanted to go into the movie business. The scarce equipment was now bought at greatly reduced prices. Many movie houses opened all over the country. And the public clamored for more and better movies.

To make better movies, the film-makers had to change from the narrow scope of recording movement to focusing attention on new techniques. Two men were primarily responsible for putting motion pictures on the road toward becoming one of the world's greatest arts: Georges Méliès and Edwin S. Porter.

While others were working with realistic movies, Méliès introduced fantasy films, and with them, almost all of the

This sketch of an early movie theater illustrates the close connection between advertising then and now. Probably all that has really changed is the price!

techniques of trick photography. In one way or another, the clever Frenchman mastered the procedures of slow and fast motion, double exposures, fades, and dissolves. There were times, however, when he was not always aware of just what he was accomplishing. Legend has it that one day when Méliès was out shooting a scene where a bus was standing, his camera jammed. After fixing the machine, he continued shooting. Later, when the film was developed and projected, the bus magically turned into a hearse. Actually what had happened was that while the camera was being readjusted, the bus had left the scene and a hearse had parked in its place. When the shooting resumed, the hearse was in the bus's spot. Some say this is how stop motion photography was born.

Besides increasing the length and types of films, Méliès also revolutionized one important way of telling stories in the movies. In the past, the passage of time was recorded exactly as it occurred in real life. For example, if an actor took thirty seconds to walk from one part of the stage to another, the movies showed all thirty seconds. Now Méliès demonstrated that you could record the beginning of an action and then switch to another action without showing how the change took place. To put it another way, Méliès taught others how you could distort time. A minute could become an hour, or a century could be shortened to a second. These procedures delighted as well as mystified audiences everywhere.

At the same time the delightful Frenchman was performing his magic feats on films, a projectionist working for Edison asked for some free time to study the editing experiments going on in England and Germany as well as Méliès' camera techniques. Edwin S. Porter's research resulted in his noticing a major problem in telling movie stories: both camera and action remained constant. He recognized, for instance, that the Frenchman's films seemed to be a series of startling acts rather than a series of scenes narrating a single story. Porter began to experiment with a smoother way of joining the

Scenes from Edwin Porter's *The Great Train Robbery*. In the first scene, the desperado forces the engineer to uncouple the locomotive from the rest of the train. In the next two shots, typical Westerners enjoy a square dance. Then some wise guys spy a "tenderfoot" and force him to do a jig as they shoot bullets dangerously near his feet.

THE BETTMANN ARCHIVE

various shots and scenes together. Then in 1903, his history-making movie, *The Great Train Robbery*, demonstrated the great value of "cutting." The film itself was about western bad men who hold up a mail train, the gathering of a posse, the chase and final destruction of the desperadoes. But the eight-minute movie established first of all the value of going directly from one shot to another shot without using any titles or tricks and relying purely on the basis of the story's logic. Second and even more amazing at the time, Porter revealed that a series of scenes did not need to follow a chronological pattern alone, but might also have a dramatic sequence. The audience saw, for example, the bad men riding away from the mail train, and following that, the gagged and tied telegraph operator being rescued by his daughter. This cross-cutting of two actions taking place at the same time—parallel editing—clearly suggested the possibilities for narrative movies, rather than just recording movement. Furthermore, this great pioneer film director established that you could combine studio scenes with outdoor shots by editing different bits of film. And, finally, Porter's work hinted at the various ways the camera itself could be tilted up and down.

Thus, by 1904, the movie industry was beginning to take shape. Profits were increasing, pictures were improving and production was in full swing.

Now, Edison finally realized what a blunder he had made.

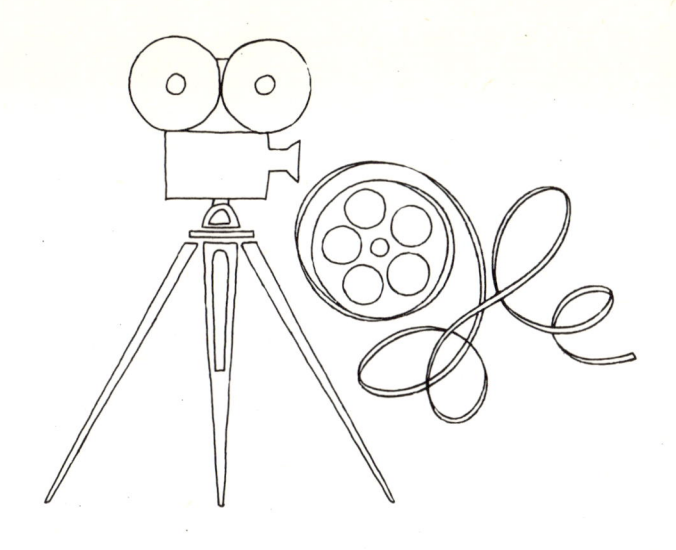

A TRUST CREATED

As the movie industry continued to grow rapidly, the major groups found their problems increasing in number and complexity. In attempting to solve their difficulties, the producers set many of the patterns for the motion pictures of today.

One problem was the distribution of films. For years exhibitors had been buying black and white prints at so many pennies per foot, ten cents more for colored pictures. Then they would trade their prints with other theater owners so that movie programs could be changed to meet public demand for variety. But this procedure was clumsy and ineffective. Some clever businessmen decided that a good solution would be to create film exchanges. The job of the exchange would be to buy films from the producers and then rent the films to the theater owners at less than a third of the purchase price. It seemed like a good idea, and in many respects it was. The film-makers could sell their pictures quickly and to a single distributor. The exhibitors could change their programs daily because of reduced overhead expenses. Everyone made money on the set-up.

But film exchanges had certain drawbacks. One such drawback was picture priority, or more commonly called *runs*: which theater got to show the movie first. Should it be by the size of theater, its location, or who paid the most money? Usually, money was the deciding factor.

Another drawback was a contract system of distribution, which forced the theater owner to exhibit only a single producer's films: block booking. In one case, an exhibitor had to rent many bad films in order to get one good movie. The other case was for each producing company to have its own theaters.

The exhibitors had further problems with the distribution arrangements. Some producers refused permission to exhibit their pictures unless the producer's equipment was used as well. That in itself would not have been bad if the equipment was not so inferior. Many times the enforced projectors literally fell apart, and audiences turned into screaming mobs.

A third problem developed as a result of the rivalry between film exchanges. Often competitors hired men called *toadies*. These thugs got jobs in another company's factory and then proceeded to destroy prints, disrupt deliveries, and damage production procedures.

One problem led to another. By now, certain elements in society were beginning to attack movies for their so-called harmful effects. Local businessmen, for example, argued that movie theaters ruined the neighborhood by raising real estate values while also attracting undesirable and noisy crowds. Another argument was the fact that many of the movies were shown in unsafe buildings. The critics pointed to several disasters where hundreds of people had been burned to death in a movie theater fire.

The biggest complaint made, however, concerned the morality of the pictures themselves. Religious and civic groups argued that the young and the foolish were being led astray by evil men with evil pictures. The outcries became so great at one point that the mayor of New York City in 1909 closed all the movie houses for a brief period. Everywhere, censorship boards appeared to judge the movies before the public would be allowed to see them. No one could explain to these well-meaning citizens that a society's morality was reflected rather than found in the movies.

In the meantime there was still the problem of who controlled the patents, and thus the entire film industry. Edison decided to settle the issue. He started lawsuits against his rivals. One by one the small outlaw companies began to disappear. They were no match for his legal force. An example of Edison's power was his ability to actually chase the Lumière corporation off American soil. The story goes that in order to save their stock from pursuing lawmen, the French representatives carried armfuls of film into a waiting boat and remained in neutral waters until they were picked up by a passing ship which was headed to Europe. The Lumière brothers after that episode decided to manufacture their equipment at home.

The first major patent test came in 1906, when the court declared that the popular Lumière motion picture machinery was copied from Edison's. For the moment, everyone had to pay him royalties. It seemed as if other court decisions would also go in Edison's favor.

But one company, Biograph, had enlisted the services of the inventors themselves: Dickson, Armat and Woodville Latham. (One sad comment was that Latham, who had done so much for the industry, agreed to testify for Biograph because the company promised him a weekly pension of thirty dollars.) Biograph claimed it owned the patents now and not Edison. Competitors took heart with the fight and the court trials dragged on. The legal fees were enormous.

By 1908, the whole situation was still unsettled and Edison was unable to stop his competition. Over a hundred film exchanges had been established in almost every major city in the United States and in key cities of Europe. Thousands upon thousands of movie houses were demanding more motion pictures. And the major corporations were fighting with each other rather than taking advantage of the situation.

In December of that year, a business meeting was held for the nine principal parties (Edison and Biograph included) who owned the important rights to the equipment and processes. To stop the squabbling, they agreed to join together to form a trust called the Motion Pictures Patents Company, which, briefly stated, established certain rules for the motion picture business. First, no one outside the organization could construct, sell, or use equipment legally for the manufacturing of movies. Second, only the Trust could license film exchanges. Third, no independent films could be shown by theaters who used the Trust's equipment or products. And fourth, eight thousand movie houses throughout the country had to pay the Trust two dollars a week if they wanted to stay in business.

Only one major figure in that meeting refused to go along with the group's decision: Méliès. From then on, the master film magician declined in importance, finally winding up his days in a home for the poor.

There was much the Trust did that was good for the industry. Film stock improved. Projectors were installed with better motors and better lenses, thereby upgrading the quality of projection. Picture deliveries were safeguarded.

The theaters were given orders to clean up their messy places. Ventilating systems were installed. Refreshments were no longer sold in the aisles. Chairs took the place of backless benches. Ushers began to wear fancy, braided uniforms. Orchestras and giant pipe organs played music to accompany the silent pictures. Soloists sang popular songs between reels. And in the very deluxe theaters, stage curtains were drawn at the conclusion of each major picture to signal the end of a performance and the start of another. Thus, the theaters tried to become respectable.

Early movie house interior with audience and piano player. A Keystone film of 1913 is shown on the screen.
THE BETTMANN ARCHIVE

The greatest change from the point of view of the manufacturers of movies came in production procedures themselves. By now, the industry began to employ a host of people to make pictures: directors, performers, script writers, set designers, and publicity agents. Something had to be done to make their combined efforts successful. The answer came in the form of a producer-controlled studio.

No one illustrates better what this means than Thomas H. Ince. By 1914, the little known director had taken it into his head to stabilize the carefree and slipshod factory methods of the filmmaking process. In his studio and on his lot, his standardization of film production became law: start with a good story, map out every detail in a shooting script, assign a director to implement, not interpret, the script; and leave Ince alone in the editing room. No matter what the movie was about—usually they were westerns starring William S. Hart—Ince pictures shared the producer's trademark of realism, clarity, and action. For them and for him, the method was fine. But the film business never understood that nothing was ever good for everyone.

To put into effect standardized production designs, large studios were soon erected. In place of the old factory operation, new stages were constructed, plush offices for executives were installed, adequate storage facilities for props, costumes, and processing equipment were built. Movie making was big time, and only those with money seemed to be able to survive.

This attempt at standardizing procedures was a fatal mistake for the Trust. Obviously, the independents did not have the money or organization to compete with such mass production procedures. They were forced to think of new means for getting the public to see their pictures instead of the Trust's.

The solution was not long in coming: experiment with different types of movies. By making every picture the same, the Trust discouraged any experimenting. The independents, at first, turned to making motion pictures based on the classics, starring famous actors.

The decision to film the great novels and plays rested upon a number of reasons. First, the method had been tried in France with mixed results. Financially it had flopped. Artistically, it was weak. But psychologically, *Film d'Art*, as the movement was called, created an atmosphere of respectability for movies. Now the elite, the wealthy, and the educated were drawn to the silent screen. Now, too, producers recognized that the stuff of movies could go beyond cheap melodrama. Another reason was that Sarah Bernhardt, the great stage actress of the day, had made a four-reel movie called *Queen Elizabeth* which an independent film producer, Adolph Zukor,

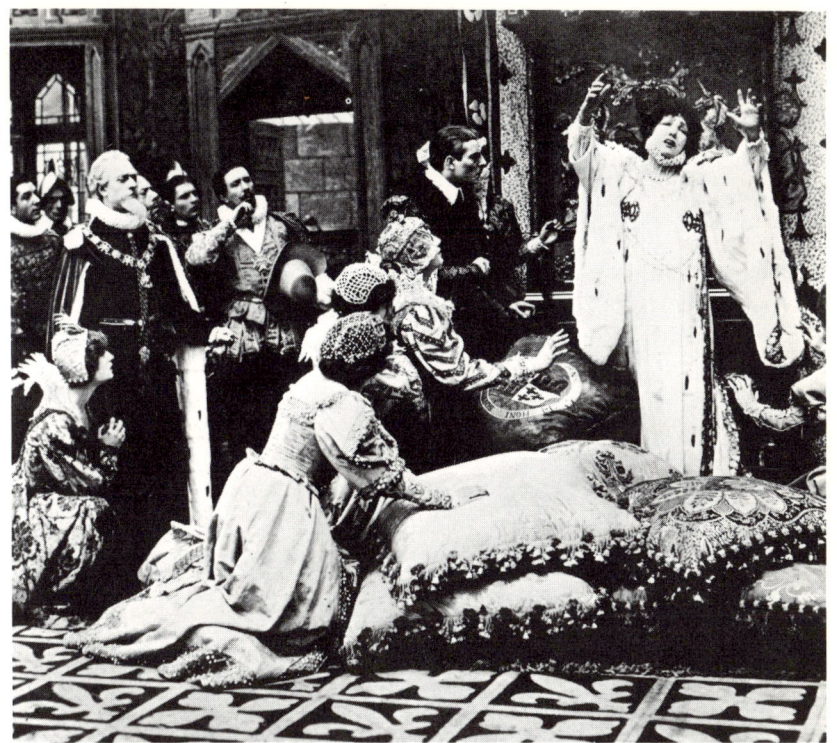

Adolph Zukor demonstrated his uncanny business skill when he imported the French film *Queen Elizabeth*, starring Sarah Bernhardt. American audiences liked the idea of showing famous players in famous plays.
THE MUSEUM OF MODERN ART/FILM STILLS ARCHIVE

had successfully imported to the United States. So overwhelming was this picture's success that Zukor decided to form a new company, Famous Players in Famous Plays (later to become Paramount Pictures).

There was a third reason: the power of money. Carl Laemmle, nicknamed the "Little Giant of Kenosha," had formed an organization called the Independent Motion Picture Company (IMP). His attitude was if we don't have it, then we'll buy it. A case in point was a young girl working for Biograph, a member of the Trust. To audiences around the world, she was known as the "Biograph girl." By promising her more money and her name in lights, he was able to bring Florence Lawrence, the first film star, to IMP pictures. Zukor lured Edwin Porter to his camp with the same tactics. The Trust began to lose its status.

In essence, the outlaw companies, as some called them, made feature films of more than one reel. And as the pictures became longer, the subject matter became wider in scope. Even more significant, talented performers and artists, who had found themselves working in what they considered to be an inferior medium, were eager to improve the quality of the movies.

The movie war was on again.

THE FIRST GIANTS

In spite of the commercial battles, movies had undergone some phenomenal successes during their fifteen-year growth and emerged as the fifth largest industry in the United States. New York was no longer the center of film production. From coast to coast, and continent to continent, people, in spite of the Trust's threats, were making movies according to a popular pattern.

The themes films centered on were the wishes of the underprivileged: laughter, love, make-believe and adventure. Usually, the emphasis was related to society's woes: the hardships of poverty, the evil of liquor, the poor working girl being molested by her boss, the sinful price connected with material success, and the heartlessness of the rich.

In each movie, three characters were always present: the hero, the heroine, and the villain. The hero was portrayed as

Lillian Gish in *Romola*, an Italian historical costume movie of the mid 1920's.

THE BETTMANN ARCHIVE

a handsome young man who believed in all virtuous things but because of his poverty, he began to waver. Always, however, his character enabled him to overcome his temptations.

The heroine, too, was virtuous, good-looking, and young. She fought for the underdog and resisted the evil suggestions of wicked men. In addition, this lovely lady presented an image of charm and excitement. She was meant to represent what each innocent man dreamed of as the ideal sweetheart.

In comparison with the beautiful people, the villain was made to look ugly and symbolize all that was bad in society. Usually the evil man came from Europe, the large city, or the wealthy class. He had every vice known to man. Everyone was in danger as a result of the villain's actions. But by the end of the movie, the hero had put an end to the sinister being, and had won his sweetheart's love.

When these formula movies began, the names of the people who played the major roles were not listed. The producers realized that if a certain performer became popular, he would demand more money. And more than anything else, the movie companies wanted to keep costs down.

But soon the public started asking for motion pictures which starred lovely, curly-haired blonde girls. In satisfying the movie audience's wishes, the producers found that Laemmle's method worked: pictures which featured a certain player made the most money. Thus they began to publicize performers. The star system was born.

Of all the great and memorable stars of that era, Douglas Fairbanks, Sr., best symbolized the all-American boy: charm, good humor, excitement, athletic skill and undying optimism. Picture after picture portrayed him in some daring feat of strength coupled with whimsical attacks on the popular ideas of the day. In one picture, for example, he mocked the pacifism of the period. In another, he ridiculed publicity hounds. But always, Fairbanks did it with grace and flair. No one seemed

Douglas Fairbank, Sr., the gay, optimistic hero in the face of danger, in the 1924 historical film, *The Thief of Bagdad*.
THE BETTMANN ARCHIVE

Mary Pickford in the little-girl pose that made her America's sweetheart.

THE BETTMANN ARCHIVE

to mind when Fairbanks turned away from the camera or covered his face when any real acting was necessary. The audience enjoyed his continuous motion, his excellent pace and brisk mannerism. The star's great showmanship more than made up for his limited acting skill.

For the female side of the story, there was the dream girl. No one has ever enjoyed more lasting popularity or been more commonly called the "American sweetheart" than the beautiful, curly-haired blonde, Mary Pickford. Millions of moviegoers the world over were in love with the talented star who cried, suffered, and fought through the early reels, turning down the advances of wealthy but spoiled men. But when the movie was over, Little Mary, who symbolized virtue, love, and innocence, showed that all the trouble was worth the rewards of the good life. Her generation saw in Mary Pickford the ideal woman.

The importance of the stars cannot be emphasized enough. For the most part they were ones who made the difference between which picture succeeded or failed, which studio gained a stronghold in the industry or was put out of business.

The birth of movie stars also gave rise to large advertising campaigns which tried, in many cases successfully, to create images which were then continuously reinforced by publicity departments. In those days, the lives of stars were not distinguished from their movie lives. Athletic stars, for example, gave advice on how to stay physically fit. Movie queens counseled young girls on ways to become popular. To a large degree, movies were helping shape a nation's image.

No man made more stars in those early years than Mack Sennett. While other directors were making westerns, romances, and adventures, Sennett concentrated his skills on developing stars for the most popular of American film types: comedies.

If anyone could turn out pictures quickly, Sennett could. He needed no scripts, just a simple situation where two men

The famous Keystone Cops as they appeared in the 1913 movie, *In the Clutches of a Gang.* Note how Sennett emphasized the physical features of his players.

THE BETTMANN ARCHIVE

could eventually get into an argument: for instance, a bum and a policeman; an employee and his boss. From that pattern, he added one gag after another, always emphasizing the physical and psychological traits of the performers. Then, when all the filming was done, Sennett would edit the raw pictures (rushes) into a superbly timed comedy.

In this connection, his greatest contribution to movies might well have been the discovery of an English pantomimist: Charles Chaplin. One night, so the story goes, Sennett went to a vaudeville theater in hope of finding new talent for motion

Charlie Chaplin and his unforgettable tramp costume.
THE BETTMANN ARCHIVE

pictures. He became interested in a "little Englisher" dressed in a frock coat acting the part of a drunk. Weeks later, in California, after having trouble with a particular star, Sennett decided to get a replacement and wanted the little fellow in the limey makeup and costume. He contacted his New York agents and asked them to get in touch with a comic, whose name he had forgotten—something like "Chapman" or "Champion." The orders were to pay the man $150 a week to sign. Within three years, the Englishman would ask for a million-dollar contract.

Sennett encouraged Chaplin to develop his own screen personality. Step by step the greatest clown of them all added physical features to his idea of a bum who wanted above all else to attain human dignity: baggy pants, a silly mustache, a foolish face, oversized shoes, a gentleman's walking stick, and a comical walk. In the decades that were to follow, Chaplin's portrayal of the little tramp touched the hearts of people the world over. When Charlie succeeded in winning a battle, audiences felt it was their success. And when Charlie failed but was unwilling to concede defeat, men and women from all corners of the earth were moved to tears.

By 1914, American film-makers and their stars had captured half the movie market of the sixty thousand cinemas in the world; the United States had over 25 percent of the actual movie houses. The pattern of big business had been firmly established: large studios, a star system, fantastic expenses, and standardized pictures.

With unlimited opportunities more apparent than ever before, members of the Trust became concerned with their individual dreams rather than their common cause. And the Motion Picture Patents Company was doomed.

In particular, there was the issue of experimentation. The bigwigs wanted conformity, but the men of genius wanted freedom. The conflict was crucial to the career of an outstanding director who refined all that had been learned in the brief history of movies: David Wark Griffith.

This brilliant man understood that there was an art to making movies: editing and technique. In the past, the concern was on plot and stars. Now he argued it should be on style.

For a number of years, he had tried to understand the basic elements of film making. Griffith knew by 1914 what no one else was to know until his masterpiece was released a year later. He would then teach the world that cameras and film are foremost in importance, not stars; that movies must be made according to the skill of the artist, not the financial whims of the businessman. Furthermore, Griffith would demonstrate that the essence of every film is in the individual shots. The way in which they are set up, filmed and edited will determine the quality of the motion picture.

But in 1914, many of the producers thought him mad. They were not about to give him money to make longer and costlier motion pictures. They did everything possible to discourage his experiments. So Griffith left New York and went west to California where he got a job that would allow him more freedom to work. By chance, he read a cheap novel which suggested to him an undertaking of such magnitude that if successful would revolutionize the movie industry. The picture would be a history of the Civil War and the aftermath of that tragic event which gave rise to the Ku Klux Klan.

Together with his great cameraman Billy Bitzer, he began shooting on July 4 and continued until October 30, 1914, the longest filming of a single movie to date. It cost five times more than any other motion picture previously made; originally ran for close to three hours (thirteen reels) and included the basic principles of all movies to come.

On February 8, 1915, *The Clansman* opened in Los Angeles, California. The audience was shocked. Griffith had created unbelievable effects: battle scenes resembling popular Civil War photographs, the ride of the clansmen as seen from a moving car. Every known camera technique was used to create movie art: close-ups, long shots, the iris, the mask, and split screen shots. The acting was the most realistic yet seen on the screen. It was a sensational achievement.

The people were shocked for other reasons as well. Whether Griffith intended it or not, the members of the Ku Klux Klan were shown as heros for suppressing the blacks. And the only good Negroes in the film were those who remained faithful to their southern masters. Showings of the film resulted in riots and storms of protest.

Griffith had done the impossible. Whether you agreed or not with his philosophy of the Civil War, you had to agree that he made men see movies as never before. The title of the film was changed to *The Birth of a Nation* and President Woodrow

A balloting scene from the highly controversial Reconstruction episode in *The Birth of A Nation*.
THE BETTMANN ARCHIVE

41

To appreciate the enormous undertaking that *Intolerance* presented to Griffith in 1915, examine this shot from the Babylonian period in the movie. Notice how four thousand players are spread out on balconies, at great distances (look through the arches), and on numerous steps.

CULVER PICTURES, INC.

Wilson summed up a nation's opinion: "It's like writing history with lightning."

But the artistic and commercial success of *The Birth of a Nation* did not satisfy Griffith's wounded pride. Shocked, angered and hurt, the great director was determined that those who accused him of prejudice and racism would be answered. So it was that he began in 1915 to make his longest, costliest, and probably his greatest motion picture: *Intolerance*.

The theme of the movie concerned the bigotry and injustice that had been thrust upon mankind down through the ages. His argument was that only through love, friendship, and charity can we hope to survive.

In order to make this point, Griffith conceived of four stories which would be told at the same time, yet woven together by the symbol of an eternal mother sitting by her cradle, endlessly rocking.

The modern story told about social injustice inflicted upon a poor family, mainly because of the actions of self-designed do-gooders. A second story had to do with the overthrow of ancient Babylon, principally because of a jealous priest's treachery. A third narrative told of the massacre of the Huguenots, the result of a cruel and vicious queen mother's revenge. And the fourth tale dealt with the story of Jesus Christ, murdered by men frightened of his teachings.

In this massive film, Griffith used every camera technique of the day to create marvelous moods, exciting action, and spectacular sets. By composing each shot, building from that into scenes, and then to sequences, D. W. Griffith demonstrated the art of the silent film.

Yet, the public was bewildered. They could not follow what was happening. Griffith lost almost all his money. All he had to show in the end—for his pride, his purpose, and his time—was one of the greatest movies in motion picture history.

THE CHANGING TIMES

As a result of World War I, the motion picture industry was clearly divided into two major groups: those who were mainly interested in making money and those who wanted to develop the art of the film.

Hollywood became the place where the money-makers migrated. Why? One reason was California's climate. In the early days, producing films in Brooklyn and West Orange limited the number of pictures that a corporation could make outside the studio. Now, with the growing emphasis on exciting, fast-moving outdoor movies, the producers needed a place with year-round sunshine and wide-open spaces. Hollywood was ideal.

A second reason that the United States, and in particular Hollywood, became the movie capital of the world after the war was because most of Europe's movie industry had been destroyed. America's film production grew in a haven of safety and security while foreign competition struggled just to stay alive.

The third reason, and probably the most important, for Hollywood's control lay in the fact that the cinema was a second home for many people. They went to the theaters on a weekly basis and expected to see a different program each time. No other country could supply the exhibitors regularly except the American film industry.

So the large studios grew even larger in California. The great stars continued to move west and the producers turned their thoughts toward the multi-billion dollar business of supplying the world with popular films.

By this time, the producers had figured out a unique and new way to get youngsters to the movie theater every Saturday: the serial. These were ten-minute stories with a terrifying ending which left the hero or heroine in great danger. He might be in a ship sinking at sea. Or she might be tied to a log, being drawn to a buzz saw. What happened? To find out, you had to wait a full week. Sometimes, the whole serial took fifteen weeks to finish. And then a new one took its place.

But for the adults, the chaos of war had changed their tastes. No longer did they find satisfaction in innocent blonde girls, or clever men who found hope by criticizing contemporary problems with a joke. Fairbanks, for example, survived the switch in audience expectations by using his philosophy and prowess in films depicting historical times. Thus, for almost a decade more, the ego-building symbol of male filmgoers swam, fought, and loved in such movies as *The Mark of Zorro, The Three Musketeers,* and *The Thief of Bagdad.*

New stars appeared, however, to reflect more adequately the era. One such person was Rudolph Valentino, the Latin lover who symbolized the non-smiling, aggressive, and passionate male. Another was Theda Bara, dubbed "the vamp,"

Rudolph Valentino romancing Vilma Banky in the 1926 adventure, *Son of the Sheik*.

THE BETTMANN ARCHIVE

who represented the post-war woman: sexy, spoiled, brunette, and dangerous. To love her was to seal your own destruction. The emphasis was clearly on fast living and good times.

The major director of the period from 1918 to 1923 was Cecil B. DeMille. He had no particular artistic talent. He inspired no individual performer. But he had an uncanny sense of the audience's mentality. His philosophy was to give the public what it wanted: sex, splendor, and sensation. Art was replaced with relevancy. Flashy clothes, exotic gestures, and sumptuous surroundings interested his fans more than a story with significance and a film with quality. So successful was DeMille in satisfying the movie-goers that most of the surrounding studios imitated his methods and materials. Hollywood was raking the money in.

The lives of the stars, the directors, and the producers were truly incredible. These film people got to believe their own publicity which portrayed them as gods and goddesses. The result was that the big shots lived as if money meant nothing. They had rambling estates, solid gold bathtubs, numerous cars, and fantastic wardrobes.

In spite of Hollywood's money and popularity, the great artistic developments for the next decade came from Europe, in particular from Germany and Russia.

Germany's films, as the films of all nations now and then, reflected her problems as well as her dreams. These were the days in which Germans were awakening momentarily from a horrible dream only to return to a nightmare more monstrous than the first. It was a time when people wandered among ruins confused, tormented, and hungry.

This was the time when Germany's once great film industry that had supplied thousands of European cinemas with quality products began to gather new strength as a giant in the field. Studio after studio reappeared. In particular, the actors, directors, technicians, and producers were attracted to one mammoth studio: UFA. This semi-monopolistic organization set its goal on removing any obstacle to the success of artistic German films.

This was also the time when -*ism* concepts of art—Cub*ism*, Dada*ism*, surreal*ism*, and expression*ism*—appeared to symbolize the meaning of what was going on in Europe. To explain briefly, these theories changed the purpose of art from showing the outwardly familiar to revealing what one felt about the familiar. The -ism artists were trying to reach an audience's emotions by arranging the various parts of a work of art to communicate a mood rather than a reproduction of actual events.

Before long, Germany's pitiful situation, the new art, and the ambitious industry became united. In the motion pictures from 1919 to 1928, the audience found society fragmented, performers abrupt and phantomlike, and the stories centered on violence, injustice, sadism, and death. While Hollywood exploited sex the German movies argued that erotic love and passion were dangerous and destructive.

Nowhere was the connection between film production and the values of a society more clearly seen than in the revolutionary movie of 1919, *The Cabinet of Doctor Caligari*, a story based upon a madman's nightmare. Everything in the film was designed to represent the fantastic dream-world this insane man lived in. The streets and buildings were arranged in twisted shapes and forms. The film's lighting emphasized shadows and darkness. The acting dramatized the strange and unnatural ways of disturbed thought and action. Throughout the movie, the audience witnessed the marvelous interweaving of plot, setting, acting, and camera technique to create a psychological movie.

Germany's film-makers also felt a need to revive a nation's pride in her past. So her famous directors turned their attention for a while to movies about great heroes of folklore and myth. The stories of young lovers fighting heroically against death on massive sets were extremely popular both on the

A scene from the expressionist film *The Cabinet of Doctor Caligari*, starring Werner Krauss as the menacing magician doctor.

THE BETTMANN ARCHIVE

continent and in the United States. (Fairbanks, as a case in point, imitated a great deal from these medieval productions.)

Another example of Germany's film school was the emphasis upon the brutal, dirty lives that millions of poverty-stricken Germans had to endure. In movies appropriately classified as "street scenes," the producers went to great extremes to show how decent, good people were forced by unfortunate conditions to live lives of crime and despair.

A very important development in German movies, in addition to the historical, psychological, and brutal motion

49

pictures, was the emphasis on good scripts and excellent technical standards, as well as on popular stars. The credit for this significant contribution goes not only to the great screen writer Carl Mayer but also to the brilliant cameraman, Karl Freund. Together these two men, working with outstanding German directors, established the value of the moving camera, which Griffith had already tried in *Intolerance*.

Although movie shots in the past had shown a variety of camera positions, these creative film masters experimented with imaginative ways of moving the cameras towards and away from their subjects, as well as up and down. Let us examine briefly their technique as used in a memorable movie of 1924, *The Last Laugh*. This story about a proud,

A scene from the German movie *The Last Laugh*. The original version ended with Emil Janning as an aging doorman reduced to scrubbing the floor in the bathroom. The film's American distributors wanted a happier ending, however, so an unexpected inheritance comes to the washroom attendant.

THE BETTMANN ARCHIVE

aging hotel doorman who is demoted to toilet duties was filmed without the use of subtitles. Early in the film, to illustrate a point, they mounted a camera on a tricycle, placed the device in an elevator, and began shooting. The effect was to have the audience think it was riding the elevator and (as the tricycle was rolled through the revolving hotel door) walking through the lobby and outside onto the street. Another example was the attempt to express what the old man felt when he was drunk. This time they strapped a portable camera to his chest, and had the star wobble about the set. This particular method of showing action from the point of view of the person himself became known as "the subjective camera."

After a while, the German film-makers built a reputation that attracted the attention of Hollywood's moguls. One by one the great directors, the great stars, the great technicians were lured to the West Coast to make money. And when they left Germany, the great UFA began to falter, waver and finally collapse. In years to come, one by one the exploited and disillusioned artists returned to their homeland. They could not make their kind of movies and their disappointment over Hollywood's crass commercial system was only surpassed by the horror of Germany's new repulsive morality in the image of Adolf Hitler.

THE RUSSIAN WORKSHOP

Even more dramatic than the different production methods of Germans and Americans was the new school of film-making just getting under way in the Soviet Union.

During the days before the 1917 Bolshevik Revolution, the Russian film industry had remained a backward and primitive organization. While other nations, recognizing the entertainment and economic values of movies, encouraged business growth, the czarist regime seemed indifferent. In short, only a few production companies, run by foreign businessmen, produced, distributed, and exhibited movies in over a thousand cinemas across the vast stretch of Russian land. Even more astonishing was the fact that all movie equipment and raw film stock had to be imported.

The leaders of the revolution decided to do something about this state of affairs.

To the Soviets, it was not enough that movies were entertaining (as the Americans emphasized) or subjective (as the Germans demonstrated). Here was a country whose people had just undergone what to them was a heroic revolution. One year after that unforgettable uprising in 1917, Lenin, their leader, said: "For us, the most important of all the arts is cinema, and the cinema must and shall become the foremost cultural weapon of the proletariat." To achieve that end, Lenin ordered the Commissariat of Education to supervise the production of all Russian films.

Most significant was the decision by the Kremlin to nationalize the motion picture industry. Nothing could have been worse for the foreigners running the business. One by one they fled the country, taking with them the tools of their trade. So great was their malice that the film-makers hid or destroyed whatever equipment or film stock they could not carry. Virtually nothing of value remained.

To counter such measures and also to train a new crop of directors and technicians favorable to Russian-Marxist ideas, the Soviets set up a number of cinematography schools. From 1918 to 1923, the problems in teaching, studying, and making movies were tremendous. First, very little raw film to shoot pictures existed and there was little hope that the stock would be replenished. (The war prevented foreign trade for years to come.) Second, electrical service was seriously disrupted by the political events. This resulted in a huge number of studios and cinemas closing down. Third, not many teachers were available. And fourth, there were few movies of any quality that the inexperienced students could see. The one exception was Griffith's *Intolerance*, which became the chief textbook of the film schools. In later years, many of the great directors would credit Griffith with influencing every Russian movie made from 1920 to 1930.

Fortunately for world cinema, the young men's desire for knowledge was greater than the limitations of their educational surroundings. These apprentices, with almost no technical or artistic background, began speculating and testing the various ways shots could be cut, pictures composed, and values communicated.

The underlying purpose of all film study and production was dictated by the government: make movies which will circulate among the Russian people and the world the aims and virtues of Marxist-Communism. Every film-maker was measured by his ability to teach, to convince, and to influence his audience of the greatness of the new Soviet order.

Newsreel production became the first task of the rising movie-makers. One reason for this was the limited film supply. Longer pictures were not financially practical until 1923. In addition, since the studios were bare and poorly lit, outdoor shooting seemed more sensible. But most important, special trips were arranged by the government to carry communication men to the war front to collect material for agitation and propaganda purposes behind the lines.

The agit-trips, as they were sometimes called, produced amazing results. Not only did the students learn how to handle their equipment, but more significantly, they advanced original methods of editing the exposed film footage. There was a special reason for this. In order to make propaganda pictures, the exposed shots had to be rearranged rather than just joined together. Thus, as Griffith's work had suggested, cutting became the key to "message" movies.

Call it what you may, the policies were somewhat similar to those of many Hollywood producers. The artist did what he was told or else he couldn't work. The purpose was to sell a product to the people. The Americans were pushing entertainment, the Russians ideology.

Yet, as is always the case with talented men, there were artists who found a way to live with the system and yet create masterpieces. No greater example can be found in the history of Russian cinema than Sergei Eisenstein, who came to the movies from a theatrical background. He wanted to make people see as they had never seen before. Eisenstein believed, as did Griffith, that the greatness of film lay in editing rather than in a moving camera.

Working with other important directors, Eisenstein emphasized a revolutionary concept of editing: *montage.* Based on his study of psychology and the Japanese language, the great director pointed out that a new meaning could be obtained from a movie's shots by rearranging their relationship to each other. By placing a picture of water, for example, next to a shot of salt, you could create the idea of a tear. But we are going a little too quickly. Let's back up for a moment.

The great Russian film teacher of the academies, Lev Kuleshov, had taught the young artists two valuable insights into a shot: (1) each shot had a meaning of its own, and (2) the meaning of that shot could be changed by the position of the shot in the actual movie itself. Even more important, by changing the position of a shot in the film, you could change the emotional effect connected with that shot.

To illustrate the technique, Kuleshov took a shot of a man's face which showed no emotion at all. Then he experimented with editing and a live audience. The first time he showed the film he combined the shot of the man with a shot of a soup bowl on a table. The second time he replaced the soup shot with a shot of a dead woman in a coffin. And the third time, the casket shot was replaced with the shot of a girl playing with her toy bear. His audience had no idea of what was being tested. They cheered the actor's ability. To them, he looked hungry in the shot with the soup bowl, deeply moved in the casket scene, and pleased with the youngster at play. In reality, however, the man had never seen any of the three events. Furthermore, his face had not changed in any of the shots. Editing had created the emotion.

Next in importance came the work of Kuleshov's excellent student Vsevolod I. Pudovkin. For the pupil, the master's method of editing meant symbolism. What Pudovkin did in addition to arranging each shot carefully was to intercut two shots which were different but when placed together gave a special meaning to each other. One of the most famous examples of the method was his 1926 film *Mother*. This was a story of a woman in the days of the Czar who in trying to protect her son, an enemy of the State, from capture by the police, unknowingly gives his whereabouts away. The mother's mistake brings about both her son's death and an understanding of what her son was fighting for. As the film comes to an end, the mother is standing among the bodies of slain prisoners, her son included. Soldiers are mounting their horses to ride down the remaining people. The mother raises the red flag and faces the soldiers. The order is given to charge. She is killed. But the last sequence of the film includes several dissolves of chimneys and rooftops with the final shot of the red flag waving in the sun. In short, the flag symbolized the fact that the Soviets would eventually win over the forces of the Czar.

Of necessity, Pudovkin stuck to the party line: (1) always have your heroes represent the masses rather than an isolated individual; (2) always defend the working class no matter what; and (3) always make things appear better than they are, thereby suggesting a glorious future for the Soviet citizen. Yet, in his movies, this intelligent director was able to create moving and sensitive images in stories about the people. Because of this particular quality of his work Pudovkin is often referred to as Russia's film poet.

And thus we come to Eisenstein. He rejected emphasizing a story line, sub-plots, individual heroes and professional actors. If montage can cause such profound feelings, he preferred to have his movies get their meaning by the arranging of the shots. For him, the hero would be the people; the story, the revolution; and the enemy, the Czarist regime. For his actors (except in the major parts), he wanted everyday people—the comfortable and the deprived, the old and the young. And his main job was to edit the various shots in such a way that not only would the story get told, but the audience would be *shocked* by what it saw.

He worked with what some have called "iron shooting scripts." Everything was controlled: shots, lighting, and acting. But most important, in the editing process, Eisenstein created the exact rhythm necessary to get the shock effect he wanted. When he wanted the audience to feel fear, for example, the shots were held for a long time on the screen. When he wanted to change the mood, the shots moved quickly and were filmed from different angles.

Probably the most famous example of Eisenstein's technique was in his 1925 film *The Battleship Potemkin*. The

A massacre scene on the Odessa steps from Eisenstein's *Battleship Potemkin*.

THE BETTMANN ARCHIVE

purpose of the picture is propaganda: to justify the revolt of sailors in 1905 and their attempt at overthrowing the tyranny of the Czarist regime. In brief, the story involves the rebellion of a battleship's crew against the superior officers because of infected rations; the death of the crew's leader and the sympathetic reaction of the citizens of Odessa; the cruel retaliation by the Czar's troops against the people, and the eventual showdown between the battleship and the warships of the fleet.

The movie begins with balanced shots of the ocean breaking against the shore, switches to the gentle swaying of the sailor's hammocks, and builds to a confrontation between the crew and the officers. Eisenstein deliberately depicts movement from shot to shot as well as in the frame itself. To him, the film's meaning was established by the pace of the action as well as by the joining together of contrasting shots. Each gesture, shot, and period of projection was carefully controlled.

Toward the end of the film, the director has a scene near a large, wide outdoor stairway called the Odessa Steps. Two kinds of people are shown reacting to the rebellious sailors: those who favor the Czar and those who encourage the sailors. Suddenly Czarist troops arrive and walk slowly down the steps shooting, stabbing, and killing anyone in their way.

Eisenstein's technique of rhythm, symbolism, and cutting created an emotional impact that at first was confusing to his Russian masters and the audience in general. Interestingly, the film received recognition in the Soviet Union only after it began to be banned outside Russia.

Before Stalin put an end to the experimental program begun by the early leaders of the film schools, the film-makers of the Soviet Union developed the techniques for a new type of movie experience, one that would contribute greatly to the course of motion picture history.

THE MAD GENIUSES

The people of the world were witness to fantastic social, economic, and political revolutions in the nineteen-twenties. Rebellion seemed the order of the day. Nothing was sacred. No one knew what would fall next or how long it would be before normality returned. The tensions, feelings, and reactions of that topsy-turvy era were best seen, for our purposes, in the unusual movies being made in Paris and in Hollywood.

In the French quarters, a small group of film artists gathered to make motion pictures that pleased themselves rather than satisfied the desires of producers, distributors, exhibitors, and middle-class audiences. Their tastes were very different from what the public had come to expect from the commercial cinema. For the most part, they did away with concrete plots, beautiful stars, and clear-cut moral lessons. Instead, the new directors sought to reveal man's subconscious. There was no attempt to interpret or criticize the findings; the purpose of the movie was to show the inner mind as it was. (You might remember that interpreting man's innermost thoughts was a preoccupation at UFA in Germany.)

Sometimes the absurd, illogical movies could reflect humorous and original points of view. René Clair, a novelist turned movie-director, made a film comedy of the absurd called *Entre'acte* (1924), which defies a detailed description. His purpose, in short, was to amuse his audience by showing unusual visual images: a cannon doing a dance, a man being killed by a clay-pipe gun, and a dancer with attractive legs, a black beard and a pince-nez. Even more startling was the sequence that begins with a camel pulling a hearse. Soon the dignity of the procession is disrupted as the camel goes one way, the hearse the other with the mourners running in hot pursuit. Finally, the coffin falls off the carriage, the corpse rises, magically vaporizes the mourners, and disappears himself. You might recognize some of the sight gags and chase episodes of the Mack Sennett School, which Clair greatly admired along with Chaplin's motion pictures. However, the Frenchman went further in depth and technique. Clair's stylistic power, then and throughout his illustrious career, rested on an ingenious talent for cutting, pacing, and farcical drama.

Not all the absurd films, however, were quite so humorous. Just the opposite is true. Luis Buñuel, for example, made *Un Chien Andalou*, or *The Andalusian Dog* (1929) which, at the time, was the extreme in shocking the sensibilities of the spectator. This savage and brutal movie shows such scenes as a young woman's eye sliced in two by a man using a razor, and dead donkeys sprawled over two grand pianos. For the most part, these dream images suggested to the viewers the revulsion that the young intellectual felt, not only about the world in general, but about the horrible state of affairs in his Spanish homeland.

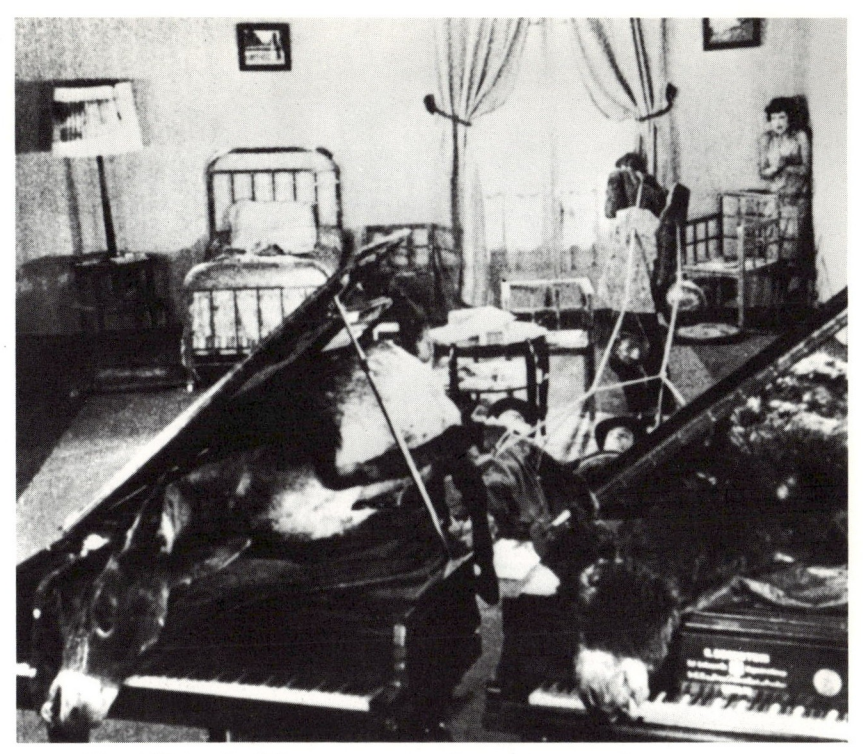

Un Chien Andalou is an excellent attempt by artists to destroy existing film conventions and open up the screen for shocking new techniques and themes, as illustrated here by the two donkeys in the pianos.

HERMAN G. WEINBERG COLLECTION

Within this Paris community there was another alien, Carl Dreyer, who came from Denmark. Dreyer had come to break with the everyday, matter-of-fact procedures of film-making. Since the early 1900's, directors had used the camera to symbolize, to shock, to amuse, to teach, and to influence the audience. Now Dreyer saw another use: a microscopic view of mankind.

He decided to make a motion picture, emphasizing cutting and camera techniques, that would give the public a close-up of life: *The Passion of Joan of Arc* (1929). Unlike his fellow artists in Paris, Dreyer showed the external world by selecting

The gifted actress Falconetti portrays the imprisoned French girl holding a mock crown of thorns given to her by the English jailers in Dreyer's *The Passion of Joan of Arc*.

CULVER PICTURES, INC.

The youthful Swedish star in the role that brought her to Hollywood: Greta Garbo as Countess Elizabeth Dohana in *The Story of Gosta Berling*.

CULVER PICTURES, INC.

sensitive shots of the human players, the inanimate but significant objects, and the contrast between pale monastery walls and the shadow-like features of Joan and her religious persecutors. The story was limited to the last day of the "witch" trial, and the young, innocent girl's burning at the stake. Slowly, painfully so, the film records her suffering, her anguish, and her faith. The total effect of the film is overwhelming. Dreyer continued to make movies for decades to come, but none surpassed this early cinematic masterpiece.

Hollywood greedily watched the work of the Germans, Russians, and French. What was liked was bought: pictures and personalities. What wasn't for sale was imitated.

But the greatest American foreign import of the day was from Sweden. That beautiful land had, for a few golden years —1914-1924—developed a fine collection of films. One in particular caught the eye of producer Louis B. Mayer: Mauritz Stiller's *The Story of Gosta Berling* (1923). The movie was about the trials and tribulations of a defrocked priest who fought for understanding against prejudice, for truth against deceit, and for tolerance against injustice. Costa's cause is helped considerably by his love for a bewitching countess. The actress who played the part was Greta Garbo. When Mayer brought her to the United States two years later, she was an instant sensation. Garbo, with her stern glances, inventive use of make-up, taunting mannerisms and natural beauty, became the symbol of desirable womanhood. Most unusual for the place and the time was that Garbo achieved her superstar status with ability, taste, and dignity.

With all the attention on foreign talent and large expenditures, Hollywood tried but failed to utilize properly three of the greatest American directors of the age: Erich von Stroheim, Joseph von Sternberg, and Robert Flaherty.

Stroheim was Stroheim. In everyday language, he was honest, relentless, tough, uncompromising, and sarcastic. As a result, very few people could work with the exacting director.

Erich von Stroheim (1885-1957) in his typical pose as the cynical Prussian officer.

THE BETTMANN ARCHIVE

But those who did worked with the best. Hardly any of the eight films he directed were finished by him. Stroheim made movies to satisfy his realistic and artistic ambitions. The producers wanted to confine his films to normal production channels which just wasn't possible.

The classic story of the proud rebel began when he was working for Laemmle's Universal Pictures on a movie entitled *Merry-Go-Round*, a tale about lustful days in sinful Vienna (a favorite Stroheim theme). The great director, with his usual intense desire for realism, was ordering monogrammed underwear for the extras who played Austrian soldiers, just so they could feel regal. It didn't bother him that the soldiers would always be photographed fully dressed. Irving Thalberg, a young producer who was later to become a great figure in motion picture circles, got fed up with Stroheim's techniques. Upon hearing that the director was spending several days drilling the same extras on how to salute Austrian officers, Thalberg fired Stroheim.

Someone else finished *The Merry-Go-Round* and Stroheim went to work for Sam Goldwyn. This time the picture was *Greed*, a film version of Frank Norris' novel *McTeague*, a story about a man destroyed by his lust for money. Stroheim took the cast on location and came back with fifty completed reels, almost ten hours of movie. The studio said it was too long. So Stroheim cut it to twenty-four reels, four hours of film. Meanwhile, Goldwyn joined studios with Louis B. Mayer of Metro, and the new M-G-M operation hired young Mr. Thalberg as one of the major producers. Thalberg fired Stroheim again, and someone else edited *Greed*. When the film was finally released, it received the same fate as *Intolerance*. Not many people understood Stroheim's cynical and ironic treatment of man's lustful nature. In short, Stroheim made movies like no one else. And because he was different, he could not succeed in Hollywood.

Von Stroheim symbolically depicts in this famous wedding party in *Greed* how incompatible the young bride (Zasu Pitts) will be with her coarse husband (Gibson Gowland). Eventually, the lust for money reduces the couple to an animal-like existence.

CULVER PICTURES, INC.

Stroheim was also an extremely fine actor, particularly in the role of a stern, authoritarian, cynical scoundrel. Even after he was refused directorial duties, Stroheim continued to act in films, contributing some of the screen's finest acting performances.

Another proud rebel of the time was Joseph von Sternberg. This great artist's skillful lighting techniques in his limited number of movies conjured up romantic and emotional settings which even today provide extraordinary experiences for the audience. In addition, Sternberg was famous for the way in which he filmed women, particularly the beautiful Marlene Dietrich. Although the talent was there, Sternberg was limited by poor production policies which emphasized stories and stars rather than his pictorial composition.

Still one more artist who could not compromise with incompetent producers or accept low film standards was Robert Flaherty. For him, motion pictures meant the opportunity to capture the reality of man's majestic struggle with nature. The way in which Flaherty edited his raw films into a new and creative experience for the audience earned him the title "father of the documentary film." He used no studios, no stars, no prearranged stories. Instead he traveled to northern

A scene from the first major documentary film, Robert Flaherty's *Nanook of the North* (1922), a dramatized account of the Eskimo's struggle for existence.

THE BETTMANN ARCHIVE

Canada where his first great film *Nanook of the North* told of the Eskimo's hard life and to the South Seas where the beautiful movie *Moana* revealed the romance of a native culture. Again, Hollywood had little use for such an artist.

Small wonder then that the world puzzled at the strange goings-on in the movie capital of the world. The art of the movie had reached a new height, and those film directors who elevated it were not commercially manageable.

THE SILENT HOURS

These then were the early days when pictures began to move. It was the period before television, when radio was still young, and the idea of rocketing to the moon was only science fiction. A new art had been created for citizens the world over regardless of age or education, color or creed, wealth or poverty. It was the result of long, hard work and creative thinking by thousands of people from all over the world.

Most of what we know today is based upon those silent hours when large studios were built, familiar movie patterns were established, and great stars were born. The film-makers' talents provided a rich heritage for all by using their noisy machines to project motion pictures onto a flimsy screen in a makeshift, messy theater. Looking back on those exciting times, we can see it as an age of triumph and tragedy, of love and laughter, of czars and tycoons.

The greatest star of them all.

THE BETTMANN ARCHIVE

But very few movie giants were happy in the late twenties. All that they had built was being threatened by the possibility of talking pictures. They feared that the coming of sound would spell disaster for the industry.

The silent film died when movies began to speak in 1927. The "talkies" were a great success and the motion picture industry once again embarked on a grand new era in entertainment history.

BIBLIOGRAPHY

The author hopes that the following selective book list will aid the interested reader in exploring more fully what happened when pictures began to move. Because of this book's brevity, no one writer's opinions were singled out and for that reason references to specific authors have not been given. Anyone reading the following books which your author has consulted will have no difficulty in determining which books were made use of, what was taken from them, and where we each went our own way.

Bainbridge, John. *Garbo.* New York: Doubleday, 1955.

Barry, Iris. *D. W. Griffith: American Film Master.* New York: Museum of Modern Art, 1940.

Blum, Daniel. *A Pictorial History of the Silent Screen.* New York: Putnam, 1953.

Cahn, William. *The Laugh Makers: A Pictorial History of American Comedians.* New York: G. P. Putnam and Sons, 1957.

Ceram, C. W. *Archaeology of the Cinema.* New York: Harcourt, Brace and World, 1965.

Crowther, Bosley. *The Great Films: Fifty Golden Years of Motion Pictures.* New York: G. P. Putnam and Sons, 1967.

──────. *Hollywood Rajah: The Life and Times of Louis B. Mayer.* New York: Holt, Rinehart & Winston, 1960.

──────. *The Lion's Share.* New York: Dutton, 1957.

DeMille, Cecil B. *Autobiography.* Edited by Donald Hayne. Englewood Cliffs: Prentice-Hall, 1959.

DeMille, William. *Hollywood Saga.* New York: Dutton, 1939.

Eisenstein, Sergei. *Film Form and Film Sense.* Edited and translated by Jay Leyda. New York: Meridian Books, Inc., 1957.

Everson, William K. *The American Movie.* New York: Atheneum, 1963.

_____. *The Bad Guys: A Pictorial History of the Movie Villain.* New York: Citadel Press, 1964.

Franklin, Joe. *Classics of the Silent Screen.* New York: Bramhall House, 1959.

Griffith, Richard. *Samuel Goldwyn, The Producer and His Films.* New York: Museum of Modern Art, 1956.

_____ and Arthur Mayer. *The Movies.* New York: Simon and Schuster, 1957.

Hall, Ben M. *The Best Remaining Seats.* New York: N. Potter, 1962.

Hart, William S. *My Life East and West.* New York: Houghton Mifflin, 1929.

Huaco, George A. *The Sociology of Film Art.* New York: Harcourt, Brace & World, 1965.

Huff, Theodore. *Charlie Chaplin.* New York: Schuman, 1951.

Jacobs, Lewis (ed.). *Introduction to the Art of the Movies.* New York: Noonday Press, 1960.

Knight, Arthur. *The Liveliest Art.* New York: Macmillan, 1957.

Lahue, Kalton C. *Continued Next Week: A History of the Moving Picture Serial.* Norman: University of Oklahoma Press, 1964.

Lindgren, Ernest. *The Art of the Film.* New York: Vista Books, 1960.

MacGowan, Kenneth. *Behind the Screen: The History and Techniques of the Movies.* New York: Delacorte Press, 1965.

Morin, Edgar. *The Stars.* New York: John Calder, 1960.

Nicoll, Allardyce. *Film and Theater.* New York: Thomas Y. Crowell, 1936.

O'Leary, Liam. *The Silent Cinema.* London: The Chaucer Press, 1965.

Pudovkin, V. I. *Film Technique and Film Acting.* Translated by Ivor Montagu. New York: Lear, 1954.

Ramsaye, Terry. *A Million and One Nights: A History of the Motion Pictures Through 1925.* New York: Simon and Schuster, 1964.

Schickel, Richard. *Movies: The History of an Art and an Institution.* New York: Basic Books, 1964.

Sennett, Mack. *King of Comedy.* Edited by Cameron Shipp. Garden City: Doubleday, 1954.

Seton, Marie. *Sergei M. Eisenstein: A Biography.* London: The Bodley Head, 1952.

Taylor, Deems, *et al. A Pictorial History of the Movies.* New York: Simon and Schuster, 1943.

Tyler, Parker. *Classics of the Foreign Film.* New York: Bonanza Books, 1962.

INDEX

advertising campaigns, 36
agit-trips, 54
Armat, Thomas, 10, 25
Bara, Theda, 45, 47
Battleship Potemkin, The, 57–58
Bernhardt, Sarah, 28–29
bicycling, 16, 18
Biograph, 25–26, 29–30
Birth of a Nation, The, 41,43
Black Maria, The, 12–13
block booking, 24
Buñuel, Luis, 60
Cabinet of Doctor Caligari, The, 48
camera technique, 13–14, 51
cameras, 6, 9–10
celluloid film, 7, 10
censorship, 24
Chaplin, Charles, 37, 39, 60
chasers, 18

Clair, René, 60
cross-cutting, 22
Daguerre, Louis Jacques Mandé, 5–6
daguerreotype, 5–6
DeMille, Cecil B., 47
Dickson, William, 8, 25
distribution, 23–24, 26
Dreyer, Carl, 61–62
duping, 16
Eastman, George, 7
Edison, Thomas, 8, 10–11, 12, 14, 16, 22, 25–26
editing, 20, 22, 40–41
Eisenstein, Sergei, 54–58
Entre'acte, 60
exhibition, 16, 18, 24, 26, 39
Fairbanks, Douglas, Sr., 33, 36, 45, 49
Famous Players in Famous Plays, 29

film costs, 12, 14, 18, 40
Film d'Art, 28
film exchanges, 23–26
film length, 13, 20, 40
film technique, 20, 22, 36–37, 40–41, 43, 47, 54–58, 59–62, 67–69
film time, 20
film types, 20, 31, 33, 36–37, 45, 48–50, 54–58
Flaherty, Robert, 64, 68–69
Freund, Karl, 50
Garbo, Greta, 64
Germany, 47–52
Goldwyn, Sam, 66
Goodwin, Reverend Hannibal Williston, 7
Great Train Robbery, The, 22
Greed, 66
Griffith, David Wark, 39–41, 43, 54
Hart, William S., 28
Hollywood, 44–45, 48, 51, 54, 64
Ince, Thomas H., 27–28
intermittent motion, 8–10
IMP, 29–30
Intolerance, 43, 53, 66
Isaacs, John D., 6
Jenkins, Charles Francis, 10
Kinetoscope, 8–9
Kircher, Father Athanasius, 2
Kuleshov, Lev, 55
Laemmle, Carl, 29–30, 33, 66
Last Laugh, The, 50
Latham family, 9–10, 25
Latham loop, 9–10
Lawrence, Florence, 29–30
Lumière, Auguste and Louis, 10, 16, 25
Marey, Étienne-Jules, 6–7
Mayer, Carl, 50
Mayer, Louis B., 64, 66
Méliès, Georges, 18, 20, 26
Merry-Go-Round, The, 66
Moana, 69
Montage, 55

Motion Pictures Patents Company, 26–30, 31, 39
Muybridge, Eadweard, 6
Nanook of the North, 69
Nickelodeons, 16
Niépce, Joseph Nicéphore, 5
Paramount Pictures, 29
Passion of Joan of Arc, The, 61–62
penny arcades, 8
persistence of vision, 3–4, 6, 10
photography, 5–7, 20
Pickford, Mary, 36
Plateau, Joseph Antoine Ferdinand, 3–4, 6
Porter, Edwin S., 18, 20, 21, 22, 30
producers, 8, 10–11, 12, 14, 16, 23–27, 44–45, 53–54
projection, 2–5, 8–10, 14
projectors, 8–10, 18
Pudovkin, Vsevolod I., 55–56
Queen Elizabeth, 28
Roget, Peter Mark, 3
runs, 24
Russia, 52–58
Sennett, Mack, 36–37, 39, 60
serials, 45
shots, 20, 41
star system, 29–30, 33, 47
Stiller, Mauritz, 64
stop motion photography, 20
Story of Gosta Berling, The, 64
studios, 12, 27–28, 47
Thalberg, Irving, 66
theater, 14
toadies, 24
UFA, 47–52
Un Chien Andalou, 60
Valentino, Rudolph, 45
Vitascope, 10–11
Von Stampfer, Simon Ritter, 3–4
Von Sternberg, Joseph, 64, 67–68
Von Stroheim, Erich, 64, 66–67
zoetrope, 4
Zukor, Adolph, 28–29